DISGUSTING ANIMAL DINNERS

Leeches Eat Blood!

Miriam Coleman

PowerKiDS press™

New York

Published in 2014 by The Rosen Publishing Group, Inc.
29 East 21st Street, New York, NY 10010

First Edition

Editor: Joanne Randolph
Book Design: Kate Vlachos

Photo Credits: Cover, p. 14 sydeen/Shutterstock.com; Front Cover (series title) © iStockphoto/lishenjun; Back Cover (graphic) -Albachiaraa-/Shutterstock.com; pp. 5, 8, 9, 16 iStockphoto/Thinkstock; p. 6 Auscape/Contributor/Universal Images Group/Getty Images; p. 7 Przemyslaw Wasilewski/Shutterstock.com; p. 10 kurt_G/Shutterstock.com; p. 11 Pakhnyushcha/Shutterstock.com; pp. 12–13 Edward Kinsman/Photo Researchers/Getty Images; p. 15 Frank Greenaway/Dorling Kindersley/Getty Images; p. 17 Scientifica/Visuals Unlimited/Getty Images; p. 18 Visuals Unlimited, Inc./Dr. Robert Calentine/Getty Images; p. 19 Paul Reeves Photography/Shutterstock.com; p. 20 Mircea Bezergheanu/Shutterstock.com; p. 21 Bridgeman Art Library/The Bridgeman Art Library/Getty Images; p. 22 Louise Murray/age fotostock/Getty Images.

Library of Congress Cataloging-in-Publication Data

Coleman, Miriam, author.
  Leeches eat blood! / by Miriam Coleman. — First edition.
    pages cm. — (Disgusting animal dinners)
  Includes index.
  ISBN 978-1-4777-2881-9 (library binding) — ISBN 978-1-4777-2967-0 (pbk.) —
ISBN 978-1-4777-3041-6 (6-pack)
  1. Leeches—Juvenile literature. I. Title.
  QL391.A6C65 2014
  592'.66—dc23
                                          2013018984

Manufactured in the United States of America

CPSIA Compliance Information: Batch #W14PK6: For Further Information contact Rosen Publishing, New York, New York at 1-800-237-9932

CONTENTS

Meet the Leech

What did you eat for dinner yesterday? Maybe you had pizza or chicken, with ice cream for dessert. Human beings enjoy a whole range of different foods. What about eating blood, though? Most humans would say, "No, thanks!" Not all animals would.

Leeches are a type of worm that often feeds on blood. Eating blood might sound disgusting to you, but a leech probably wouldn't enjoy ice cream. Not every animal enjoys the same foods that we do. Different animals' bodies are adapted to get their **nutrition** from different sources. Just as we have flat teeth to help us chew up that pizza, many leeches have special mouths that make them good at sucking blood.

Some leeches will suck the blood from most any mammal, such as a person, that gets close enough for them to attach themselves. Others prefer to feed on the blood of fish, waterbirds, or many other animals.

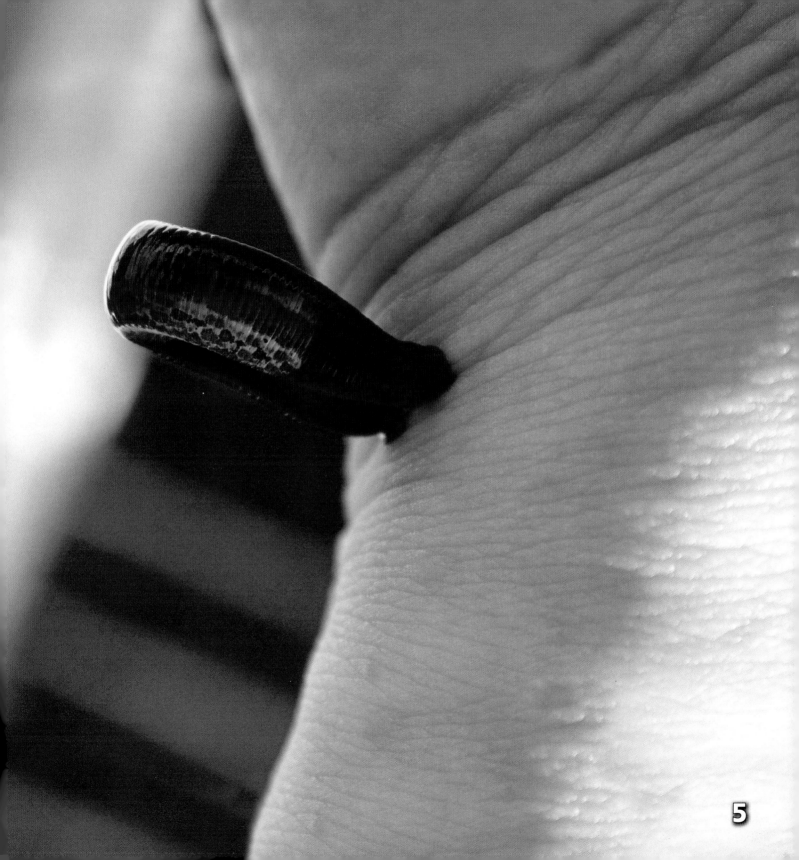

Where, Oh Where Are the Leeches?

Leeches can be found all over the world. They live in Europe, North America, South America, Africa, and Asia.

Leeches can live in different kinds of water. Most live in freshwater, such as ponds and lakes. Some types of leeches live in the ocean.

This is a terrestrial leech, which means it lives on land. There are many land leeches around the world, though some of the most common are found in Japan and India.

A pond like this is a typical habitat for aquatic leeches.

A few kinds of leeches even live on damp land, such as **rain forests**, but most are **aquatic** animals. Some types of leeches are amphibious, which means that they can live on land and water. These leeches live part of the year in soil and under stones.

So Many Leeches

This leech makes its home in the shallow waters of a pond. It will eat small invertebrates, or animals without backbones, that live in the pond.

There are more than 600 different species, or types, of leeches. Different species of leeches have different needs, and so they live in different **habitats** and have different ways of eating different kinds of foods.

Leeches like *Erpobdella testacea* prefer living in freshwater with little oxygen, and so they grow in shallow, swampy waters with lots of **decaying** plants. *Piscicola geometra* like more oxygen in the water, and so they live in fast-flowing streams and on the shores of lakes where waves crash.

Terrestrial leeches use their sucking mouthparts to help them move along leaves and other matter as they search for food.

Leech Bodies

Leeches belong to a phylum, or group, of worms called Annelida. "Annelida" means "ringed," and the animals in this group all have bodies that are divided into ringed parts, called segments. The earthworms that you dig up in your garden are also members of this phylum.

Though it is hard to see their eyes, leeches do have them. The number of eyes is different for different species.

It is easy to see the segmented body of this earthworm. Earthworms are annelids, just as leeches are.

The leech has a wide, flat body with 34 segments. On each end of the leech is a sucker, which the leech uses to eat as well as move. Leeches can be black, dark brown, or green. Some have spots or stripes, while others are plain. They can measure less than 1 inch (2.5 cm) or be more than 1 foot (30 cm) long.

DISGUSTING LEECH FACTS!

1 The world's largest leech is the Amazon leech, which can reach up to 18 inches (46 cm) long. Some leeches can bite all the way through the tough hide of a hippopotamus. Some types of leeches can swallow 10 times their own weight in one meal.

2 One species of leech that lives in the Amazon likes to live up in people's noses.

3 One species of leech lives on the gums of the Nile crocodile.

4 Leeches have poor eyesight. They find their food by sensing movement or by following their sense of smell or taste.

5 People who are drinking water can accidentally swallow some types of leeches that live in rivers in Africa. If this happens, the leech can latch on in the mouth, nose, or throat and feed on the person from the inside.

6 Tiny leeches that live in rivers can also burrow into the eyes of swimmers.

Born to Suck

A leech's mouth is in the center of its rear sucker. Different species of leeches have different types of mouths.

Some leeches have jaws with sharp teeth like little saws. They use their teeth to bite into their prey, making a wound from which they suck blood.

Once a leech attaches to its host, it puts a special chemical into the wound so the animal will not feel the leech. It also puts something in the wound to make the blood keep flowing.

The wider end of the leech is its head. It has a sucker that it uses to move and to hold on to prey. The rear end is narrower and has a sucker for feeding.

Instead of jaws, other leeches have proboscises, which are long, sharp tubes like straws, which they stick into prey to suck the blood through.

Not all leeches eat blood, however. Some leeches have large and powerful mouths, which they use to suck in whole animals such as worms and slugs.

Blood for Lunch

Leeches feed off many kinds of animals, including turtles and other animals that share a leech's home.

When a bloodsucking species such as the freshwater leech finds some prey, it attaches itself to the animal with one of its suckers. It uses its sharp teeth to cut into the animal's skin. Then it releases a special **chemical** in its **saliva**, which numbs the wound so the host animal can't feel it.

The chemical also prevents the animal's blood from **clotting**. This means that the blood keeps flowing into the leech's mouth until it has had enough to eat. The leech will keep feeding until it is about five times its normal weight.

Some kinds of leeches leave a bite mark that is shaped like a Y.

Life Cycle of a Leech

Leeches have both male and female parts. This means that they can all lay eggs and **fertilize** the eggs of other leeches. After they mate, one leech produces several cocoons, which hold and protect the eggs. Some species of leeches carry their cocoons by attaching them to their own bodies. Most attach the cocoons to underwater plants.

This leech is carrying its eggs under its body.

Life is dangerous for leeches and their eggs. Birds, such as this Wilson's snipe, are happy to catch and eat leeches.

When they hatch from the eggs, baby leeches look just like tiny adult leeches. Some leeches live only for a few months, but others can live for several years.

Dr. Leech

Doctors have been using leeches to treat illnesses for thousands of years, going back at least to ancient Egypt. People once believed that all kinds of illnesses were caused by bad blood. Letting leeches drink plenty of a **patient**'s blood was thought to rid the body of illness. In **medieval** times, doctors used millions of leeches every year.

The most commonly used leech in medicine is *Hirudo medicinalis*, which naturally lives in Japan.

This painting from medieval times shows a doctor using leeches to treat patients.

Sometimes they let leeches drink too much of a patient's blood, which was dangerous.

Doctors still use leeches in medicine today. Because of that special chemical in their saliva, which prevents blood from clotting, leeches are helpful in certain kinds of **surgery**. They help blood keep flowing into body parts or veins that have been **damaged**.

Helpful Parasites

Leeches that eat blood are parasites. This means that they live by attaching to other animals and feeding from them. Leeches often attach themselves to fish, turtles, and ducks. Sometimes they attach themselves to people, so be careful swimming in ponds and lakes!

Although it can be nasty to find these slimy creatures sucking your blood, leeches can also be very helpful to people. Now who wants blood for dinner?

If you do find a leech attached to your body, the best way to remove it is by sliding your fingernail under the edge of the sucker to break the seal.

GLOSSARY

aquatic (uh-KWAH-tik) Living or growing in water.

chemical (KEH-mih-kul) Matter that can be mixed with other matter to cause changes.

clotting (KLAHT-ing) The thickening of a liquid.

damaged (DA-mijd) Harmed.

decaying (dih-KAY-ing) Rotting.

fertilize (FUR-tuh-lyz) To put male cells inside an egg to make babies.

habitats (HA-buh-tats) The surroundings where animals or plants naturally live.

medieval (mee-DEE-vul) Having to do with the Middle Ages, the years from AD 500 to AD 1450.

nutrition (noo-TRIH-shun) The act of getting the food that living things need to live and to grow.

patient (PAY-shent) A person getting care from a doctor.

rain forests (RAYN FOR-ests) Thick forests that receive a large amount of rain during the year.

saliva (suh-LY-vuh) The liquid in the mouth that starts to break down food and helps food slide down the throat.

surgery (SER-juh-ree) An operation.

INDEX

WEBSITES

Due to the changing nature of Internet links, PowerKids Press has developed an online list of websites related to the subject of this book. This site is updated regularly. Please use this link to access the list: www.powerkidslinks.com/dad/leeches/